LIFE
BEYOND
STRESS

LIFE
BEYOND
STRESS

MARGARET McDERMOTT

TATE PUBLISHING
AND ENTERPRISES, LLC

Published by Tate Publishing & Enterprises, LLC
127 E. Trade Center Terrace | Mustang, Oklahoma 73064 USA
1.888.361.9473 | www.tatepublishing.com

Tate Publishing is committed to excellence in the publishing industry. The company reflects the philosophy established by the founders, based on Psalm 68:11,
"The Lord gave the word and great was the company of those who published it."

Book design copyright © 2015 by Tate Publishing, LLC. All rights reserved.
Cover design by Maria Louella Mancao
Interior design by James Mensidor

Published in the United States of America

ISBN: 978-1-68142-259-6
1. Self-Help / Self-Management / Stress Management
2. Religion / Christian Life / Spiritual Growth
15.07.13

Created for you to
experience moments of reflection,
encouragement, and insight.

I dedicate this book to my dear friend Sharron Hamelin and to Mom Brunsveld. Thank you for believing in me and in what God is doing in all of our lives. Thank you for your support, love, and friendship. You both have been such a blessing and encouragement to me! Love you!

Acknowledgement

Thanks to Mike Litman for teaching that "you don't have to get it perfect, you just have to get it going!"

Thanks to Dale and Annette who started the vision by sharing their photos!

Thanks to Elaine, Janet, and all the listening ears who have been part of this journey.

Thanks to Rich and Staff at Selby Marketing for getting the original work from dreams to reality!

Thanks to Trinity, Gabriel, and the Tate Publishing team for doing the miracle work of turning what "was" into what "is," just as Jesus turned the water into wine and the storm into calm!

Thanks to Esther for accommodating the last minute request for review. A friend in need is a friend indeed!

Thanks to Miriam and Wendy for your prayers, friendship, and support. You are anchors to my soul, wind to the wings of my dreams, and two beautiful gems in the treasure chest of my life! Love you both!

Above all, thanks to God for the blessings of life, health, opportunities, insight, friends, family and divine assignments, conversations, connections, and timing which have all been part of this book being written.

Contents

Introduction

Welcome! A new journey has begun for you! This book is divided by two elements—reflection and strategy. Reflection, because the first thing needed to get beyond stress is to get the true picture of our life and ourselves! We need to shut off all the noise or find a place where we can just be still and be quiet. In our homes and society, it seems there is noise everywhere. I pass people walking along nature trails and hiking up the mountain plugged into some form of noise. They miss the orchestra of nature's song. They miss the soothing to their soul and the inspiration that comes from the beauty around them. They miss the very gift of God to connect with Him in those moments and the insightful divine wisdom that contains the answers we need.

We need to stop, sit, and ponder. For some of you reading this, you need to stop and rest. These are the first steps required to start living beyond stress. Jesus so often went to the mountain to get away from the crowds, the noise, and distraction. We can celebrate living everyday, or we can be stressed and stuck in everyday living. Stop and reflect!

Part of this book is strategic, because we also need practical direction in the form of steps and strategies to help us get to the new kind of life we want to live. If you can under-stand and apply the basic concept and strategy of this book, you will be well on your way to experiencing change and living beyond stress. One idea or one question can change your situation and the rest of your life.

May the words on these pages be a gift of freedom, change and hope to you!

Part I

Changing Course— Changing Reality

1

What is Stress?
Introduction

If you had no thoughts whatsoever, how much stress would you have?

If you couldn't think about problems, you certainly couldn't worry about them.

You certainly wouldn't get stressed about what to do with them, or how you are going to get through a situation, or how it's going to end up simply because you wouldn't have any thoughts.

The simplest definition of stress is pressure.

We often call and know pressure in our body as pain.

Pressure in our emotions or mind is known more as *stress*. When it's not dealt with, it will also burst forth out into areas of our body and life in some way, shape, or form.

When you get happy news or good news, there is no association to stress but rather to freedom. When we are happy, there is a freedom in our body. It's easy to smile, clap, sing, gesture with our hands or literally jump for joy. The ability for life, emotions, thoughts, and our body to move positively and uninhibited equals freedom.

Pressure is a sign, a warning. Yellow lights are a warning to slow down and be cautious. Red lights are an immediate signal to stop. Do not proceed at this moment. Dead-end signs mean you are at the end of the road; you can't go any further, you've hit your limit. It's time to make a decision. Pressure can be an indication of these signs and messages in your life, whether it's the pain in your body or the stress in your mind and emotions.

As in most things you want to change, it's necessary to question what the main issue is—not the symptoms, but the source.

So let's take a quick look at the dynamics of stress, and what's really going on in your life.

2

The Dynamics of Stress

Compressed air is air under pressure. It's great for filling up a balloon to celebrate or a tire so we can drive our vehicles and bikes. However, when that pressure hits a certain level, it will cause that tire or balloon to blow. We see that in some people who are stressed. They "blow" just like a tire, leaving a trail of debris where they have been.

Too much weight on a shelf can create enough pressure that it's only a matter of time until it gives way. Then everything comes tumbling down as the shelf crashes to the floor in pieces.

We see this also in people who are stressed. The weight and burdens of life, situations, relationships, and other pressures get to a certain point. They just crash as everything around them seems to come tumbling down, and they fall to pieces.

In the very core of the earth, life is moving. However, when pressure builds to a certain degree, it can explode or erupt into a volcano, earthquake, tsunami, etc. I'm sure we have all seen, if not experienced, how stress also erupts in our lives, bringing destruction, shifts, and changes.

Have you also noticed that if the pressure is not dealt with ahead of time or at the beginning, the effects and consequences are far more devastating and far-reaching than the original pressure point?

The tire that was once traveling on the road is now all over the road.

What was on the shelf is now scattered or broken all over the floor, maybe even knocking down or breaking other things it hit.

What was under the earth has now surfaced through to the earth. Likewise, the pressure that builds in us usually breaks through somehow into our spirit, soul, or body, crashing or exploding into the realm of our life.

So what can we do about it?

3

Moving Forward

As we get our thoughts to move forward, the rest of us will move forward as well.

Knowledge is only effective to the degree you use it. So get a pen and paper. Write down one or two situations, things, or people that stress you out.

1. _____.
2. _____.

Now without analyzing or filtering them, please write down all the thoughts you have about these situations, things, or people. This book is *Life Beyond Stress* because we want to eliminate stress in your life so you can live beyond it! Write down as many thoughts as you can.

_____.
_____.
_____.
_____.
_____.

You see, if I have a colony of ants in my kitchen cupboard, I want to eliminate them. I do not want to manage them. I do not want to reduce them to just a few. I do not want to move them to another area of my life. No. I want them gone!

It still means I have cupboards. I will still have to clean them at times. I may have to unclutter them at times. I may renovate them in some form. The cupboards are not the problem; the ants are the problem. So I eliminate the source.

Likewise, we may still have to work, deal with relationships, finances, and every other aspect of our life. *But* we do not need to live stressed in these areas.

How do we do that, you ask?

4

What Do You Think?

As mentioned in the introduction. If you had no thoughts about your job, home, relationships, future, finances, etc. there would be no pressure.

- There would be no stress about failing because you wouldn't have any thoughts about failing.
- There would be no stress about disappointment because you wouldn't have any thoughts of disappointment.
- There would be no stress about anyone's expectations because expectations are certain thoughts about things.
- There would be no stress emotionally, because feelings are a by-product of our thoughts, our perceptions, and our definitions.

Once you become aware of the thoughts building the pressure, then you can intercept the process. Instead of them controlling you, you can control, channel, move, and eliminate them. In turn, you control the quality of your life, experience, destination, and often the consequences that would have come from pressure and stress.

So the question is, "What do you think?"

5

Life Must Move!

If you are driving down the highway, and you see something on the side of the road that's not moving, what is your first thought? Probably, *It's dead.*

We are not taught that life is movement and yet we do know that. We know that the blood in our arteries must be able to freely move forward. If the artery is blocked or closed, there is going to be some pressure as the blood continues to press forward, creating a heart attack. Eventually it could be death if no action (movement) is taken.

Likewise, the oxygen in our lungs must be able to move. If it is blocked or closed off, it is called choking or suffocating to death if no action (movement) is taken.

I could continue with our digestive system, the different organs and processes in our body, all of which must move.

Thoughts are just as much a part of our life as our physical body. They too must move.

It is my observation that mental and emotional stress comes from thoughts that get stuck in our system and create pressure. We have certain thoughts, maybe similar to the ones you have listed. They keep going around and around in our head, *I can't handle this anymore, This is driving me crazy, I don't know what to do, This is killing me.*

These thoughts go around and around, faster and faster like lettuce in a salad spinner, building momentum and pressure. The life and juice that literally get squeezed out of the lettuce, are a representation of the results from stuck thoughts. On top of that, more thoughts keep being added into the spinner by the second. According to Dr. Caroline Leaf (a cognitive neuroscientist with a PhD in communication pathology specializing in neuropsychology), we think some thirty thousand thoughts a day. Add them into the mix of the ones already driving you nuts. No wonder we feel stressed to the max! We are not created to handle that. Our thoughts, like all other parts of our body, are to move—move forward, free flowing, not stuck, and free from pressure.

The pressure of those thoughts can squeeze the life right out of us too and into the form of high blood pressure, strokes, heart attacks, anger, depression, etc. Consider thoughts and how big a part they have in our spirit, soul, and body. They are a main part of creating our reality. We are created to move forward.

Stress relief usually involves some form of movement that relieves pressure temporarily, but if the source is not dealt with, pressure will only build again.

Screaming, shouting, smoking, drinking, eating, sleeping, shopping, having sex, exercising, journaling, taking a vacation, or any other form of movement of choice may relieve stress temporarily. However, they won't and don't stop thoughts. Those stress-thoughts will go on vacation with you, go to work with you, go to bed with you, and be there when you wake up. I personally don't know anyone whose sole purpose in life is to accommodate or cater to stress. Yet how many people constantly live in stress? It is so costly in so many ways! So let's get these thoughts moving!

6

Call the Tow Truck!

Questions *are* the answer.

Questions are the tow truck to pull you out of the ruts and ditches of life.

Questions are the tow truck to get you back on the road, where you can keep moving on and living life.

Take a look at the thoughts you wrote down about the stress in your life. The thoughts that stress us out, that build pressure and squeeze the life out of us are the ones with a period at the end of the sentence: dead end. They aren't going anywhere. There is no direction in the content of those thoughts for them to go anywhere positive.

When you start turning those thoughts into questions or start asking questions about those thoughts, you will get direction. According to the *quality* of the *questions* you ask will be the *quality of life* you live.

I like to think of the question mark when it's turned sideways as the hook, the link of the tow truck that hooks up to you and can pull you out.

Most questions start with *who*, *what*, *where*, *when*, *why* or *how*. These are always a good reference point to help you and a good place to start.

In the quality and vision of the questions you ask will be the quality of the answers and directions you get.

Asking "Why me?" deals more with the past and why you got here. The only way this question can be useful is if you then ask "What can I do about it?" That question gives you some control, choice, responsibility, and future-focused results for the issue.

Quality questions are forward-looking and help you move forward. In relationships, for instance: Where do you want the relationship to be? What would the ideal look like? Feel like? What would it take to create that? What's the first step? What works? What doesn't seem right? How can you look or move forward from where you are right now?

Question those dead-end thoughts. Question how did you get them and what makes you believe them and keep them so then you can get rid of them!

Let's take a look at how to apply this to some common thoughts that are key culprits. If you are dealing with a specific situation or issue as you read this, I would suggest getting a pen and paper so you can work through them. Write the answers down to questions that stand out to you. Looking at your thoughts and answers on paper gives you a better perspective than just keeping them internal and unexposed. Before digital cameras, when people took pictures, the film had to be developed exposing what was hidden in the dark film to actual pictures. On the film you couldn't see anything. Once it was exposed, you got the picture. You could see. As you continue reading, these following chapters are designed to do likewise for you. As you write down the answers you get from the film of your mind onto paper, it will start the developing process. The hidden details are exposed. You will get the clarity and direction you need.

7

What?

The What Question

The *what* question is one of the best tools for discovery and getting direction.

- *What am I doing here?* Define here. Where is here? Take a moment to describe where you are right now and what you are doing here. A map is absolutely no good to anyone if they don't know where they are on the map.
- *What am I thinking about this right now?* (Having awareness of your thoughts is necessary as they are the steering wheel of your life. If you don't know what you are thinking, you will not know who is steering your life or where you are going.)
- *What thought started this whole thing?* One thought is the start of a business, a relationship, a missed opportunity, any destination and every situation. When things have gone wrong in my life I can usually go back to one specific thought that was a

key factor. It can reveal motives, desires, beliefs, and controlling factors that we aren't even aware of.

- *What thoughts do I have to keep for things to stay the same?* Analyze the thoughts that accompanied you to where you are now.
- *What thoughts do I have to think for things to change?* One of the first thoughts necessary for change is the thought that there is a way for things to change. You just need to discover it.
- *What thoughts stop this from working?*

Let's see how to apply questions in a way that will bring direction and the ability to move forward.

I Don't Know What To Do

- What is the message this thought gives you?
- What is it implying?
- What is it that you don't know what to do about? What part of it do you need to deal with, change, confront, or address?
- What is needed in this situation?

You can also ask:

- What can I do?
- What would I like to do?

- If I could do anything with no restrictions of time or money, what would it be?
- What is my heart telling me?
- What do I feel at peace with?
- What don't I feel at peace with?
- What have I been noticing lately?

Let's say you don't know what to do because your co-workers are going on a weekend get-away. You don't really want to go or financially can't afford it, so you don't know what to do.

The issue is not your co-workers going away. The real issue is how and what will it take for you to say no, how you can manage to save and go another time in the future, how you can find a way to still be part of the team, have fun, maintain your finances, and most of all, still have peace. The issue could be finding a way to pull the team together to do something else you all enjoy at a different time with less expense.

I Can't Take This Anymore

- What exactly is it that you can't take? What is the real issue?
- What is it that is really bothering you about that?
- What would be the perfect scenario to you?
- In what ways do you have the ability or control to change things?

- For instance, if your job is driving you crazy, what exactly is the problem? Is it actually the work itself, the management, the co-workers, a lack of training, the amount of work, the kind of work, the pressure, the hours, the pay or something else?
- What is within your ability to change? Your approach? Communication? Education?
- What would it take to be a catalyst for change in others?
- What would it take to influence others? A conversation? A demonstration of results?

If nothing else, realize life does not stay stagnate by nature. We all have choice. Bosses can change. We can change companies. We can change positions within companies. We can change careers. We can increase education. We can start our own business. We can partner with someone else in a business.

When we make a choice, by default, we have also chosen the results or consequences.

Did you get that? Choosing a certain choice means you have *chosen* the results. They come together as in a package deal.

When you chose to drive way over the speed limit, you also just made a bad financial decision. No use complaining about the ticket, you chose it. It is the result or consequence of that choice. They go together, a package deal.

You have people in your life who don't treat you good. What do you choose? Do you choose to give them place in your life? Do you give them options? Do you choose to give them voice in your life?

If you don't change what you do about those people being in your life or how to handle them differently, then by default, they will continue to be in your life and not treat you good—package deal, your choice. What can you do, what do you need to do, and how can you do it? These are key questions to pull you out of this ditch. What are some of your options or different strategies? Do you need support to help you or prepare you to follow through with these decisions?

I Can't Do This. I'm No Good at This. I Don't Know How to Do This."

- What part of it can't you do?
- Is there a part of it that you can do, but just need help with another part?
- What would it take for you to do it? More education? Help? Tools? Time?
- What can you delegate, or who can help you?
- What will it take for you to know how to do it and be good at it?

Go back to the thoughts you wrote down. Apply some of these *what* questions to them and see what answers and directions you get. It is, for sure, that these questions will cause movement in your thinking and processing.

Other What Questions That Are Helpful

1. What Works?

When you are struggling, you need to know what does work for you. Is there a part of it that works for you? That's a message and a direction of what to keep doing, what to hold on to, and what you do want to work around. It can give you focus and encouragement that not everything is in despair.

2. What is Not Working? What Part of It is Not Working?

Maybe having a job, children, marriage, vacation, and doing certain things are all good. But there are some things involved that aren't working. It could be the time, schedule, pay, or place of the job. Maybe it's certain traits, communication, or discipline regarding the children. When you find out exactly what is not working, it is direction and a message on what you need to stop doing and where to start making some different decisions. Ask some different questions. Start focusing on the results and changes you do want—think forward, think future, think options.

3. What is the Opposite of This?

Maybe you don't know what direction to go, or what to do. But if you know the opposite, you get direction and insight.

For instance, you know you don't want to work night-shift anymore. So working day-shift would be a good option.

You can't afford eating out. What's the opposite? What are the alternatives and what would work? How about finding snacks you like and have them handy in your car, purse, or pocket? Then when you're hungry, you won't have reason to buy fast-food. Instead of meeting your friends to eat out, how about doing a potluck and you all share the cost? How about just having them over for coffee and dessert instead of a meal? This is a great question to ask when you need to find things that would work for you.

4. What is the Real Issue and Conflict?

Ask this question when you don't have peace, or life seems chaotic.

I started to have panic attacks at one point when I was twenty-five. They seemed to come at sporadic times, just out of the blue. It continued until a psychologist explained to me that behavior comes from feelings. Feelings come from thoughts; thoughts come from beliefs. I needed to discover the beliefs and thoughts that triggered the panic. They came so lightning-fast that I had to really work at catching what thought had triggered the panic. It took me one week to discover it was the word *alone*.

As soon as I thought about having to eat alone, walk down the street alone to my night shift job or dealing with finances alone, there came the panic and anxiety. Then I realized it wasn't so sporadic or out of nowhere. It was a word, a thought that triggered the panic, not a place or a person for me.

That soon came to a stop as I acknowledged, yes, I might be alone at times. "Did I have to be alone?" was the question. "No!" was the answer. What could I do? I could get a financial advisor. I could have a friend over or call a friend and go see them. Even if I was alone and attacked, I was there. I can make decisions. I can pray. If it came to the worst possible scenario, would I rather panic or die trying to be free? I would rather do whatever I could to be free. And I could always follow what I sensed in my spirit as the right thing to do at the time.

Once I started to ask questions to find what worked and then applied the answer—that took care of that. *Until you put the panic or anxiety in words, there's a lot of implied fear and vague feelings of down-and-depressed with nothing quite clear.* Take the bull by the horns and that devil by the tail. Once you expose the fear, you'll find the truth. You have a choice.

I still watch for that word when it tries to come into my awareness or mind to imply I am alone. Do I have to be alone? No! The answer is still the same. And I am still free from that anxiety years later.

If you focus on the results you don't want and don't like, instead of what is the source and what is the solution, nothing will change. You will keep living with the results. Is there a conflict because of your values or other's values? Is there a conflict because your needs or another's needs are not being met?

Being offended or being upset usually means a need is not being met. Someone doesn't feel significant, loved, heard, valued, etc. The event, word, action, or situation is often not the real issue. It's the meaning given to it. It's what is being perceived through what is said or not said. Those aspects are resolvable. It is not the end of the world. What is the real issue?

You can have a great paying job, doing what you love. However, if your highest value is family or friends, and this "great" job has you on the road all week with no time or way to connect, you are out of alignment with your deepest needs and values. That will create pressure.

Working long solitary hours by yourself with no time for social life, thinking *I'm lonely* and *I'm depressed*, is not going to do anything but build pressure and create stress. Those are dead-end thoughts with no direction. Ask, what's not working? What's the real issue? What are my needs? What is important to me?

The real issue is you need connection, so how can you start incorporating changes and opportunity for connection? Do you need to find different work, or is there a way to get your needs met in a different way that works for you? Maybe you can work around your schedule by meeting friends for breakfast before work, at coffee breaks, or during lunch mid-day. Maybe you schedule in some social time on purpose or go to the gym with a friend instead of by yourself. Maybe you schedule more time off and specifically make room and time in your life somehow for those who matter most to you! What could you adjust or change to make room and time for the changes and opportunity you need? What boundaries, or needs are not being honoured in healthy ways in your life and body? Remember that when you make choices, by default you are choosing certain results.

5. What If?

This is a great question to ask regarding your future. It is *not* a question to ask when reflecting on your past. It's a great question to turn potentially negative things into positive.

When you have unexpected decisions (future-oriented) or situations (present), asking "What if?" is a way of exploring opportunities and options.

If you feel stressed because of getting laid off or facing disappointment, here are some questions to ask:

- What if this is an opportunity to do what I haven't had time to do?
- What if I can make the changes now I've wanted to make? To travel? To start something new?
- What if this is a blessing in disguise?
- What if this is actually an answer to my prayer in some way?

- What if this is God's protection to remove me from the wrong place, time, or people?
- What if this isn't how it really appears?
- What else do I need to consider?
- *What good can come out of this?* Ask how. After there has been a fire or flood, people will search for things that would still be of value. They salvage these things by rescuing them and removing them from the situation. If a car has been totalled in a collision, it goes to the junk yard or to a salvage company. The metal frame and core parts of the car still have value and can be used or transformed into something useful. What can be salvaged from this? If you lose your job, is there a friendship that can be salvaged from that place? How about the knowledge you gained or connections you made?

These questions start to move you into hope, purpose, vision, and a freedom regarding your future if you let them. They prevent or help eliminate the stress, pressure, and frustration from dead-end thoughts about depression, failure, and disappointment.

6. What Can I Do?

This is a great question to ask when you think you are stuck. There is always something you can do. It's a great question to be proactive or when you need to make decisions and manage time.

- What can I do with someone?
- What can I do alone?
- What can I do at this time?
- What can I do where I am right now?
- What can I do with what I have, such as skills, opportunities, and abilities?

This is a good time to take inventory and ask; What do I have? I think of how many miracles involved Jesus taking something someone had and turning it into provision, or taking something and turning it around. The woman who was willing to use her bit of oil and pour it out found that it multiplied. When the wine at the wedding ran out (or maybe your contract ran out), they still had water, so Jesus used what they had. He took that water and turned it into wine. When it came to needing lunch Jesus took the two loaves and five fishes the little lad had, and with His blessing it multiplied to feed thousands. Impossible you say? No. We see this law of sowing and reaping everywhere, even in a berry bush. Plant a berry seed and you get a whole bush full of berries. However, if no one planted the berry seed, it would just sit there dormant. One berry seed wouldn't even feed a bird. But plant it and WOW! A bush full of berries will feed many birds and people for many years. So you can let what you have stay dormant or you can find something to do with what you have!

Look around and see what you have and what you are able to do. What will you do with your time? What can you do with your hands and your health? How can you make some of your possessions work for you? An oven can bake, a broom can clean. A hammer can fix things or hang things. How about your knowledge? How can that work for you?

Do you have faith? Just a little faith can move those mountains of doubt or debt – one thing at a time. When I was travelling across the country, I met a young lady putting herself through university through a dog-walking company she had started in a small resort town. She was a biologist but dog-walking was more lucrative for her – she had four staff that walked dogs for her company while she went to classes. Imagine! She got where she was because she had legs and she used them as the blessing they were. Well, I guess she had a brain and used that too, along with her legs!!! Stop, think and take inventory.

- What can I do now that I can't do later?
- What can I do to prepare for later? What's next?

Perhaps you only have one free hour. Maybe you only have ten dollars. Maybe you have a small apartment. So what?

- What can you do in an hour?

- What can you do with ten dollars? Perhaps you can buy a bus fare and go somewhere. Perhaps you can buy a snack or some groceries to make a meal or share a meal. How could you help someone else with that money?

Starting a big project may not be the thing you can or should do right now. You can spend the whole hour thinking about what needs to be done and do nothing in the end. That's frustrating and stressful. Instead, focus on what you can do with what you have right where you are.

You have certain opportunities at certain times, in certain places to do certain things. Winter in Canada usually means you can go skating, skiing, ice fishing, snowmobiling, etc., which you can't do in summer or in hot countries. So, asking "What Can I Do?" clarifies your options and opportunities. It helps you plan and manage for when you can do things effortlessly and efficiently. One hour gives you time to do some things though not everything. The language you speak enables you to do certain things.

Asking what you can do is critical in living stress free. What you can do is usually what you have control, ability, and authority over. It can be a source of stress if you keep focusing on what you don't have, what you can't do and what you think others should, can, or will do. You don't have control over them. It's even more stressful if you focus on what other people think *you* should and could do. You do have choice and control over what you do. That is one of our greatest freedoms.

7. What Does That Have To Do With It?

This is a great boundary-setting question to break certain frustrations. It helps you recognize and discover distractions and time wasters so you can stay focused, efficient.

I feel depressed. So? What does that have to do with anything? We are not our feelings. They change like the wind. That is not to be confused with the senses you get in your spirit that are warnings or direction.

I don't like that. Well, what does that have to do with anything? I may not like going to work today, but if I want my paycheck, off I go. If I want to pay my bills, take a trip or make a purchase, off to work I go. Feelings can be a deadly-and-destructive *master*, my friend.

I may not want to pay my taxes. What does that have to do with it? If I want to keep my property, then I do what I need to. What I want can be irrelevant. I'm sure some small countries do not want to fight wars, but it can be a matter of life or death for the country; a matter of freedom or dictatorship.

This question gives you guidelines for what to do regardless of distractions, feelings, opinions, and time wasters. If you are feeling pressured by other people, or perhaps someone injects an inappropriate comment into a conversation, you can use this question to keep a group focused on the real issues, topics, or events.

8. What Does That Have To Do With You?

This is similar to the above question, but is more for setting boundaries with other people.

- If you are feeling stressed, overwhelmed, or overloaded in any area of your life, relationships or responsibilities…
- If part of your stress is because someone makes decisions, but you end up paying the price…
- If someone can't pay their rent because they spent all their money at the liquor store…
- If someone thinks you are a way out for them or a free ticket in life…
- If someone lied and is upset because you won't cover for them…
- If you spend your life living out other people's expectations, demands, and commands…

I ask, what does that have to do with you?

Codependent and drama-trauma relationships can be very stressful if you think you are responsible for everything another person thinks, feels, does, or needs. Likewise, if you think someone else is responsible for everything you think, want, feel, need, or do. It's wise to challenge your thinking and beliefs on those thoughts.

I am ever so grateful to a pastor's wife who told me that just because someone needed help or money did not mean it was my job or my responsibility to do everything. Every person has opportunities, choices, and abilities, not to mention an attitude that can either help them or hinder them. Helping is healthy. However, taking on full responsibility for what is not yours, beyond your control, and what is really someone else's responsibility is *not* healthy.

What a relief for me to hear that. Sometimes, people need to help themselves by making different decisions. We do not want to enable negative behavior, choices, or lifestyles. The price is costly to all involved.

If it's not your responsibility, if your plate is full, if it's not in alignment with truth, with your values, etc., then I would suggest the answer to "What has it got to do with you?" is nothing! And if it has nothing to do with you, then you need to let go of some things. You need to let others own their responsibilities. You need to ask yourself where are the boundaries? At what point do you say no? Be aware when fear or guilt are talking; they are a separate issue that you need to address and question. Fear and guilt are your enemy, not your friends! Torment and lack of peace are their cousins. Eliminate that pressure-cooker thought that you are responsible or need to take on the needs and cares of the whole world! It doesn't mean you can't or don't help at times. You help but with healthy boundaries.

9. What's Left?

When you need to simplify, clarify, or declutter your life, ask "What's left? Is it worth it?"

- At the end of today
- At the end of your life
- At the end of your paycheck
- At the end of the conversation
- At the end of the event
- After you've bought what you wanted
- Gone where you wanted
- Done what you wanted
- When friends or family have passed on
- After you have finished your vacation
- After you have spent your time, your money, your energy
- After you have done all you could do and given all you could give

Then ask one of the following questions:

- What's left? Has it been worth it?
- What could be different?

- What brings regrets?
- What would you like to change or do different while you still can?
- Is there peace, fulfilment, accomplishment, trust, companionship, or someone who cares?
- What's going to be left at the end of the decision you're about to make?
- Is there investment, profit, or some kind of good left?
- Are you left only with emptiness? Are you left with nothing?

For those of you who are stressed because of a chaotic schedule, look at it closely. For everything you have to do, every person you have to see, everywhere you have to go, what's left?

If I take a second job, it increases my taxes, and what's left is just enough to pay the gas to go to the second job, is it worth it? I don't think so. I've been there and done that one too many times!

It's stressful to feel like we have no place, no say, and we don't make a difference. It's depressing and stressful to feel like we are nothing, have nothing, accomplished nothing, and are going nowhere.

It's stressful because that's not how we are created to live or be.

If you are in this place, then I want to encourage you that it's your time now—your time to ask some of the questions in these pages, your time to get some answers, your time to get a new direction, your time for hope to become a reality!

The positive thing is you are only questions away from finding out what works and how you can start on that path!

10. What Are You Waiting For?

If one of your dead-end, stress-producing thoughts are along the lines of: *I'm so tired, I'm stressed, I'm fed up, I've had enough, I wish, I hope, I'm waiting,* or when things are at a standstill, you might want to ask this question.

Beware of a deception if you are always waiting. *Later* never comes.

Maybe it is *who* are you waiting for?

Is what you are waiting for really someone else's job or responsibility? Based on what? Even if someone agreed to do, give, or find something for you, the point is you are still responsible for your life. Not them.

Time, my friend, is a limited resource. There are twenty-four hours in a day. No more, no less for all of us. Time waits for no man. Time can be telling you something. How long do you plan on waiting?

- What are you doing in the meantime?
- What can you be doing now while you are waiting?
- What can help you be a blessing or make a difference to others?

Remember, life becomes stressful when there is a lack of movement in any area of our life. People who are bedridden for long periods lose their strength and ability to walk and move. They lose their strength to live life to the fullest.

- What are you waiting for to make that call?
- What are you waiting for to fix something around the house?
- What are you waiting for to put the finances in order?
- What are you waiting for to finish something?
- What are you waiting for to step forward and see progress?

Are you waiting for something to happen that is not going to happen until you do something?

I can be waiting for a new job; but if I don't make any calls, talk to anyone, or send a resume, that job is not going to happen. Sometimes, what we're waiting for shows up, but we don't recognize or embrace it until there's been some cultivation, work, or effort invested. The fruit can be on a tree, but it takes work, time, and effort to pick it. It's there, but you have to do something to get it.

I have a wonderful friend in my life because on a cold winter snowy day, I saw a moving truck pull up to the house two doors down. I made a pot of coffee, got a tray, mugs, cookies, and off I went to welcome my new neighbor—a stranger, who became a neighbor, who became a friend. I can't imagine how much I would have missed in my life if she hadn't become my friend and just remained a stranger instead.

I took the opportunity as it arose. What if I waited? I'm sure we would have met at some point. But the conditions around that event started the friendship and made it memorable. What would the story be if I had waited and ended up meeting my new neighbor in frustration over an issue, in a hurry, or in a bad mood because everything was going wrong that day? How different would the results have been?

If we wait for better weather, a better time for things to be perfect, for more than enough finances, for the perfect weight, the perfect job, etc., we may be waiting a very long time. In fact, the window of opportunity may be over and the door shut. Why? **Because you are busy waiting!** The time required was spent already—spent waiting. Waiting for what? At what cost? What is it worth if you wait so long you miss it altogether?

There are times when it is appropriate to wait, such as in a full-term pregnancy. If you invest money on a term basis, it will cost you if you don't wait until that term is due. In our society, for the most part, you have to wait until a certain age before it's legal to work or drive a car. However, you need to study and practice driving before you are given your license. There are things in life that are in process, which means we need to do things while we are waiting for something else. It's when nothing is being accomplished, or we are not living the life we're created to live, that we need to start asking what we are waiting for.

At one point, I wanted to buy a webcam. I thought it was going to be very expensive, so I never even looked. Much later, I unexpectedly found one for $9.99. I was so disgusted. I could have bought one a long time ago if I had looked, instead of waiting. How many opportunities did I miss because of it?

So my question is, what are you waiting for in your life? Do you need to be waiting? Is there another issue involved such as fear, delusion, habit, wrong thinking or beliefs holding you back? What areas in your life would you like to see some progress and accomplishment? Do a double-check and see what you are waiting for.

11. What Really Matters?

When you have limits, need wisdom, need to manage time, make priorities, or put things in order, this is another effective question to ask.

It's a great question to ask when you don't know what to do, because there are so many things you need to do, want to do, or could do. It's a clarifier and can give you insight.

When all is said and done, *what* matters in the end? Based on what?

When all is said and done, *who* matters in the end? Based on what?

If you only have one hour, one day, or one month left to live, what really matters?

12. What's the Cost?

Wisdom regarding consequences, results, future, and decisions can come from asking this question. It can give you the bigger picture and value of something.

This question is necessary to keep you from making decisions that actually cost you more than you want to pay in different ways.

- What is the cost to your family?
- What is the cost to your personal time?
- What is the cost to your life span?
- What is the cost financially?
- What will it cost you emotionally?
- What will it cost you physically or health-wise?
- What will it cost you mentally?
- What will it cost you spiritually?
- What will it cost you eternally?

Spending money is one thing, as is spending time. However, what it costs may be far more than the money we paid, or the time we spent.

- What if it costs you someone's trust?
- What if the price you really pay is regret?
- What if the cost is a life sentence?

- What if your carelessness costs someone's life, as in many drinking and driving accidents?
- What is the cost of a workaholic missing their children's childhood? To the kids? To themselves?
- What is the cost of opportunities missed?
- What if the cost is your health, then your job, then your house? Homelessness?
- What if the cost is your relationships?
- What if the cost is your future?
- What is the cost of going to college or getting a career? "A lot of money!" you say.

Do you know there's a very real chance that *not* going to college *will cost you more*? The work we do, and the compensation for that work determines the very kind of life we will live.

The amount of your paycheck will determine what kind of house you can live in, where you can live, what you can do, what kind of vacations you can take, and how much time you have for vacations. It will determine what kind of interests and hobbies you can pursue. It will determine when and how you can retire. How stressful is a job wherein your hours get cut when your pay is already so low that you can barely make it? How can you ever help others if you can't help yourself?

This question is so important to eliminate stress in the long-term!

13. What's the Difference?

When making changes or choosing between things, this question can give you a reality check.

The difference between things, relationships, or decisions might be time, money, honesty, value, hope, despair, profit or loss, good or bad, big or small. How will the difference affect you? What's the difference in your lifestyle if you are debt free now but considering large monthly payments on something? The difference might be financial freedom and emotional or mental strain within a short time period.

I am not one of comparing myself to others, as all unhappiness, let alone stress, comes from comparison!

- Comparison of what you have with what you want creates discontentment and ungratefulness.
- Comparison with what others have creates envy, jealousy, hate, and lack of thankfulness.
- Comparison with what you think you should be creates inadequacy and inferiority.
- Comparison to the media's voices creates unrealistic expectations, disappointments, and illusions.
- Comparison between myself and others can create conflict, envy, strife, and bitterness.

However, there are times, in order to make the best decision between two things, that comparison is appropriate. We need to know what the difference is because we live with the consequences.

If two job offers come in, asking what the difference is, along with other *what*-questions, can help you determine what job is best for you to take. The difference between two friends determines who can help you best in a crisis. The vast difference between two different people you could marry will mean a vast difference in the kind of life you will live for the rest of your life! The difference between cars can help you determine what car is best suited to your needs, finances, and lifestyle.

So if you don't know whether to do this or that, go here or there, buy this or that, this question can help you out, along with questions like what is most important, what the cost is, etc.

14. What's Wrong? What is This? What's Wrong with This?

This is a big one when you feel worried or have a sense that something's not right, when you are uneasy about something or have a lack of peace. I personally ask this if it seems like all is going well, yet I feel heaviness, darkness, moody, or just plain yucky.

Please ask yourself this question! It can mean the difference between life and death, the right time or the wrong time, knowing if someone is the right person or wrong person. It definitely can make the difference between a good day or a terrible day.

I used to have hormone-related issues. Along with it would come a day where I felt like crying about everything. The first time or two, I wouldn't necessarily pay attention. After that, I'd think, *What is this? This isn't me.* Oh, right. Hormones! Say no more! Well, I'm not having a bad day because of you, hormones, thank you.

So I might go get some vitamins that would help. Maybe I'd have a cup of tea and just sit down to relax for a bit. My favorite music, a conversation with a favorite person, or some other comfort-giving thing would usually help to balance me out. Asking that question saved me from being just plain miserable and making everyone around me miserable. Eventually, surgery became an option I chose so I could live free from it completely.

Do not ignore these senses. Sometimes, we recognize that something is out of order. What's wrong with this picture? We can know something far sooner in our spirit than we can see, hear, or recognize it otherwise. What's wrong? What do you need to be aware? Where can you take precautions? Is it a warning of something you need to do, or something you missed?

I ask this when I felt uneasy about doing something, or being with/around someone. Please listen to those lightning-quick thoughts that something is not right. For your sake, please pay attention to what that uneasy feeling is trying to tell you.

Recently, I had such a major inner conflict because the appearances and contact I had with someone seemed so positive, yet I felt uneasy. Everything they said was true, but I kept getting this sense that something wasn't right. A later conversation confirmed a good reason for my uneasiness.

It would be similar to meeting a wonderful elderly man who just loves children. They are such a treasure, and he can't imagine life without them. In spite of what he says, something doesn't seem right. You have an uneasy sense. Later, you discover he's a pedophile. I caution parents especially that if your child is uneasy around a certain person, clings to you in panic, or goes to any lengths trying to avoid a certain person, *heed the warning!* Something is amiss. Things are *not* always what they seem. Things are not always heard, seen, or known on the surface to the human eyes, ears, or mind. Children can usually pick up more quickly on the truth and speak the truth more easily than adults who have lost the ability due to fear, being politically correct, nice, tactful, Christian or whatever else overrides those senses. Sometimes the answer is not given to us in words, but in silent actions and responses. It is still an answer.

You may not get the answers to this question right away, but asking this question acknowledges that there is something else going on. There is something else you need to know. That all is not as it seems.

How many times have you asked others, "What's wrong?"

How many times have you heard, "nothing!"?

Yet you know there is something. Ask God to show you and help you be sensitive to anything or anyone where something doesn't seem quite right. There's a message or a truth you need to know. Be willing to adapt or change as necessary until you have peace.

15. What Are My Options/Alternatives?

- When you need to expand past now, make decisions, or find a way this is a great question.
- When what you are doing isn't working, this is a great question.
- When you have to, need to, or must do something, this is a great question.

I would suggest that you do *not* filter or screen your options at first. Just write them all down or discuss all of them. One option may not be what you choose, but it may open doors to something else you would choose. While you want to go somewhere, you may find you don't have the money to pay for it as an individual; but maybe sharing makes it an option. Or perhaps there are discounted rates for early booking or a special one-day sale.

Is part of your stress because you are stuck with a dead-end thought that you can't afford it? Look outside the box of normality. Be creative. Find options. If you can't take the plane, how about the bus? What will it take for you to get unstuck and stress-free about it in a different way?

If you feel stressed regarding a large purchase, taking on big projects or in attempting to do something new, this may be the question to ask in various aspects of it.

16. What Does God Say?

This is the question to ask when you want the biggest picture, purpose, vision, insight, and wisdom. Binoculars help us see further. Microscopes help us see what is unseen to the human eye. Telescopes help us see what is far beyond us. Faith sees, believes, and comprehends what is unseen and unknown to the natural mind, ears, and eyes. There are times when God opens doors, and the impossible becomes possible, the unknown becomes known, and the unbelievable becomes reality.

God gives warnings, directions, and insight. He speaks through His Word, through others, through situations, through a check, or sense in our spirit. His warnings and guidelines are as much for our protection as when you tell a child to wait until the truck goes by before crossing the road; as much for our direction as the red light or green light at an intersection—in many cases, the intersections of our lives.

Ask God what He says, and then keep your eyes and ears open to see the answer that comes your way. What God says will help us live true and fulfilled.

17. What is The Point and The Purpose?

This question is similar to "What matters?" and "What's left?" Have you ever been in a conversation, and in spite of all the words, there doesn't seem to be a point or purpose? Worse yet, how about all the conversations with swear words that describe nothing but punctuate conversations? Is there a lack of meaningful words available? Is there nothing of value to say or share? Does the listener have nothing else to do? What's the purpose?

- What's the point of buying something you don't need, want, like, or will never use?
- What's the purpose?
- What's the point of doing what you do, going where you go, saying what you say?
- What's the purpose?

How much of your life do you spend doing things or living your life without purpose, without value, without thinking about it? How much stress does it create when you aren't living to your full potential but rather just going along with whatever, whenever, however, and whoever?

I might ask, what's the point of living in and with stress? What do you get out of it?

18. What's In Believing a Lie?

"I can't believe it!" I realized one day that every time I say that, it is *because what I think I can't believe, just happened, was just said, or just done.* So explain to me why I said that I can't believe it when it just happened!

I discovered when I say "I can't believe that," it means I don't want to believe it. It means I don't like it or don't know how to handle it. It means I don't like the decisions I might have to make because of it. Sometimes, it means I don't want to face the truth that something I believe is not true.

You watch! It's amazing to observe the tendency people have to think that because they believe something, somehow that makes it true. Maybe you tell them something, and the response is, "Well, I believe." May I ask, "What has that to do with anything? Based on what?"

Believing a lie can be a key source of stress. Wrong beliefs can blind us, limit us, and destroy us or others. Feelings and experiences can vary in different times and ways. It is important to get to the truth of the matter.

It may be convenient to believe a lie. It may make you feel better to believe a lie, but truth has a way of surfacing, like a balloon under water. Then you are unprepared and ill-equipped to deal with it. It may also come at a great cost emotionally, physically, mentally, financially, spiritually, or eternally.

It's a struggle to reframe in our minds that something isn't what we see and it isn't what we hear, and instead to trust our spirit. It's very hard to face that what we believe might not be true, that someone has been deceptive, that we've been ripped off or that someone actually wants to hurt us, especially if we've trusted them.

We struggle and try to accept, justify, deny, make excuses, take the blame ourselves and numerous other things to somehow make it right and make it okay.

I believe it's why abusive relationships continue, people continue bad habits, and we live in denial. We just can't believe it. When we find ourselves in conflict, or sensing something is wrong, we really do need to seek for the truth. We need to discover what the issue is and why we want to resist the messages that we are getting.

I do know that when we are born, we can only perceive and process in the positive. *Don't, won't,* and *can't* aren't concepts our brain can even conceive or perceive when we are born until it is trained or programmed otherwise.

When a baby wants food, they will let you know until there is some corresponding response. When a baby wants to crawl, wants down, or wants up, they make the attempt to do so. They don't stop to ask if they can. They have to be trained "Don't do that, don't touch that and don't go there." Children will pretty much *think they can do whatever they are doing* (yes, that is written correctly) and can do whatever they want to do.

It also seems we have associated *positive* as being good and *negative* as being bad. Yet, that is not necessarily true. Two negatives make a positive in math; however, if you are charging a car battery, and you put the positive cable on the wrong connection, you'll have a very negative reaction. It won't be a positive thing, even though it's positive. Unless you want to say positively dangerous!

Do you feel guilty if you believe something negative about someone even if it is true? Where do we get the idea that life is all peachy, supposed to be fair, and that we can't face the truth if it is the truth? The truth is our protection.

My book *Where Am I Going From Here? (And How Do I Get There?)* deals with what we think. The influences—and really, whose thoughts are whose, even in our own minds. If you don't know, then it's very easy to assume or think you are your thoughts.

You are *not* your thoughts or your feelings, for that matter. Some thoughts and feelings are really the voices, persuasions, influences, power of others, negative experiences, the media, society, and so forth all having something to say. Once we get clarity, then it is much easier to process what the truth, the core, the source, and the root is.

19. What Do We Need to Let Go Of?

First, realize that we do need to let go of things at times. Maybe the past, old dreams, certain people, or expectations of ourselves or others.

In order to reach something, pick up something, hold something, or do something with our hands, we have to let go of anything that takes that space or place in our hands at the moment.

Sometimes, when you let go of one thing, you end up letting go of something else effortlessly as a result as mentioned in part II of this book.

There's a time to hang on, and a time to let go. I have a picture of a tree in the fall with just two leaves hanging on it. I realized it wasn't just the leaves hanging on. They were connected to the tree by a stem. At the other end of the stem, the tree was also holding on to the leaf. The stem is similar to what we often call "strings attached" to something or someone. Guilt, control, and manipulation are things that would be good to let go of in our life. We need to be free from them, not connected to them or whatever they connect us to. Heartstrings usually refer to love and special connections, those you can hang on to. Hang on to hope, and faith too!

I remember cooking in one kitchen, and the pot handles were stainless steel with no heat-resistant protection. Not paying attention, I picked up the pot. Well, it didn't take me long to let go of that pot. Let me tell you, it was hot,

hot, hot! It burned my skin into what looked like leather instantly. *It was not hard to let go of that pot.* I didn't want the results. In other cases, it takes a while to figure out we need to let go.

20. What! Not Who!

This has become one of my favorite questions, tools, and insights in dealing with people. It eliminates stress *big time* if you can stick to the *what* of an issue rather than *who*.

Let me give you an example: *you said, you did, you always, you never.* These statements are focused on *who*. It creates blame and accusation. Instead, focus on *what* was said. Focus on *what* the person did or didn't do. Look at that issue and start asking other questions like "What is the real issue?"

Remember earlier, the example of the co-workers all going away for the weekend? The co-workers weren't the issue. The issue was that the person couldn't go or didn't want to go. It eliminates so much stress, blame, and resulting conflict.

Your teenager sneaks the keys to the car, and you get a call saying there's been a bad accident. Your teenager is in the hospital, and the car is totalled. You can focus on blaming your teenager, get mad and create more problems and stress. Or you can move forward and ask:

- What are the real issues?
- Since the car is no more, what are your options?

- What will work short term, or long term?
- How can you put these options into action?
- Do you need someone to help you?
- What is the issue with your teenager?
- What is behind the actions and thoughts?
- In your conversations later with the teenager, deal with the "what."
- Can you hear what they are saying by what they aren't saying?
- Can you hear what they aren't saying in between what they are saying?
- What is the cause of their beliefs to do what they did?
- What can you do to make sure this doesn't happen again?

You can help them work through their thought process through the following questions;

- Is what they believed true?
- What are they going to do to take responsibility?
- What needs were they trying to fill?
- How can you help them meet those needs a different way?

All these thoughts *move you forward* to answers, to the future, to prevention, and to getting to the real issue. If all your thoughts are about being mad and how you can make your teenager's life miserable, you are setting yourself up for increased stress. Worse yet, if all your thoughts are about yourself, double or triple the stress it will create. The more you think dead-end thoughts, the more stressed you'll get. *Move forward*!

If you are forever arguing with someone, *stop*! Stop and listen to *what* they are saying. Deal with *what*!

- Is it true?
- What are their feelings, needs, and values?
- What's the real issue?
- What are the options?
- What are your values?
- What can you do?
- What's the result you want?
- What do you have to do to get there?

It is just *so* much less stress to deal with the *what* and not the *who* in situations like this.

21. What Are Your Needs? What Are Your Values?

According to Tony (Anthony) Robbins we all have six basic human needs. These needs are *going to be met* one way or another. They will be met. There is a part of us that will see to it.

The reason it's hard for us to stop doing something, to start doing something, to believe something, to go somewhere or not go somewhere, etc. is that we are often getting our needs met through those ways listed. And while it may create stress or pressure to stay or keep doing those things, we may feel like we'd be more stressed if we changed and didn't get our needs met. There can be a very subtle conflict going on within us. And as with any conflict and stress, it will come out into other areas of our lives.

Remember, questions are the answer. Start to question what you are doing. How it works for you. What's the gain? What's the pain? What's the difference? What stops you? What keeps you doing the same thing?

8

How?

The *how*-questions are excellent for moving you out of stress because the very word itself implies victory and assumed accomplishment rather than failure or being a victim.

It implies there's *no* possibility of something *not* happening. It implies it will happen; it's just a matter of how. It gives hope. The first step of any journey is the very thought of it. That is true with the how-questions. It means there is a way. I just have to discover it.

- How do you want your life to be?
- How would you like this situation to turn out?
- How can you do this? What will it take? What's your first step? Who can help?
- How is this done?
- How does this work?
- How did this happen? Things don't usually just happen. It might be time to read the instructions in some cases, or the operator's manual.
- How can I learn?
- How do others do this?

- How did I get in this mess? You ask this so you get some insight, direction, and wisdom!
- How do I get out of this mess, this relationship, or this place?
- How balanced is your life?
- How can you create more balance?
- How can I make sure I never end up in this situation again?

If you look back, what were some warning signs? What were some triggers? What did you need to say no to? What did you need to pursue, say yes to, or make room for in your life?

Even if there was a disaster, you ask how it happened so you can prevent it from happening again, not so you can get in blame, anger and stress.

In crisis or in disasters such as earthquakes and tsunamis, it would be so easy to get stressed and depressed. The how-questions can get you moving into action, into your future.

- How fast can we get resources in order again?
- How can we get food, water, and shelter for people?
- How can we start to rebuild? Where do we start? Who can help? What do we have?
- How can we help effectively and make a difference?

Movement, movement, movement. I am right-handed, so when I had surgery and couldn't use my right hand, the how-question became the most popular word in my vocabulary. Tony Robbins will tell you that when you ask a question, you will get an answer. It's how we are created.

I've learned that you keep asking until you get the answer you need. How do I slice bread with one hand? The answer that worked was to wedge the loaf of bread between two heavy things so it didn't move. Then I could slice it with one hand. Sometimes I used my teeth, my leg, or my foot to assist me in doing little everyday things. It was amazing to me how creative we really are when we have to be.

How can we make it work?

I love the how-questions. They are so proactive and full of answers and potential!

9

Who?

All of us need each other in some capacity or another: a seller needs a buyer, a teacher needs a student, an employer needs an employee, relationships require someone else, a child needs a parent, as parents get older, they may need their children.

How many things or times in life, like the above list, do you require someone else? How much in your house was made, manufactured, grown, sold, and delivered by someone else so you could have it? Let me help you out. The answer is everything. Everything involves someone, somewhere, at sometime.

How does this relate to stress? Well, let me ask, how much less stress would you have in your life if you didn't have any people in your life?

On the other hand, scripture says two are better than one because if one falls, the other can help them up.

So we have stress because of some people in our life. We would also have stress if we didn't have people in our life. In some cases, the *how* and *what* questions are suitable.

However, I will note some important *who*-questions that are effective in helping us get out of the stress mode.

- Who can help me?
- Who knows about this?
- Who has experience or done this before?
- Who is "where I want to be" that has information, tips, and strategies?
- Who is the right person for the job?
- Who's in charge?
- Who has the authority to change rules, make decisions, or fix things?

For the last question, let me mention it won't be the cashier, the front desk person, the operator, or the cleaner. No use screaming at them. Now if you ask nicely, they may be able to tell you who can help you.

Have you ever been in a store and asked for something, but the employee says they don't have it? On a few occasions, I have been. I also knew they had the product. Maybe the packaging or location changed so I couldn't recognize it. I also realized the employee wasn't about to look or help. What are your choices? You can stress out, or you can realize, obviously this isn't the person who can help. So, either you ask who can help you, or you move along. If the manager or someone in authority there can't help you, then the question may be who else and where else?

Choosing to stress out isn't really an option. It won't get you the information or product you need.

10

Is There Anything Else? (And Other Questions)

There are many other questions you can ask that will be tow trucks and tools to pull you out from the ditches of stress and frustration.

Asking others what they think. Asking if there is something else. Asking for clarification or for information is smart, preventative, and proactive. Ask if you are not sure, instead of stewing and thinking you don't know, whether it's directions to go somewhere, how much something costs, or what something is.

The stress of worry is eliminated the more informed you are. Make a decision instead of worrying. If that decision doesn't end up working well, then make a different one. Remember that praying and asking God is a great way to start the process of getting the answers you need too.

Is it going to rain, snow, or shine? Not sure? Well, maybe take an umbrella and a jacket with you. Questions help you be prepared for what you need. What do you need to take in case of an emergency on the road? Diabetics will need to make sure they have insulin. Babies traveling will need diapers and bottles.

The more prepared and educated you are, the more you eliminate stress.

Are there peanuts in this? People with deadly allergies know asking that question can save their life.

Is it true? Because of fraud, cashiers often have to check large currency bills to make sure they are the real thing. It matters because there are consequences and costs to things if they are not true or real. A few years back, there was a scam where people would sell a house that wasn't theirs to sell. The new owners would discover that the person whom they paid and bought the house from wasn't the owner. The owner still lived in the house, and someone else had the money. Our lives are dependent on the truth as much as on the law of gravity. It's my observation that it's actually impossible for someone to believe a lie if they are aware that it is a lie. It's the way we are created.

Asking for help is also smart, preventative, and proactive. Asking for help with something very heavy is wise. You need your back and your shoulders for the rest of your life. Asking if the equipment has been locked down before deciding to do maintenance can mean the difference of living with or without an arm for the rest of your life.

- *Is there something I am missing?* Sometimes we may have a subtle sense that we're forgetting something or something is incomplete. Rather than continuing, why not stop and ask this question? By asking the question, you pause long enough so answers have a chance to surface rather than getting down the road and then remembering.

- *Is there still part of my dream alive?* Is there still a chance or way for this to work out? Is there something to be salvaged from this? These questions are the questions of second chance.

When I missed my bus one morning, I had to wait a long time for the next one going that route. It was cold and snowy. I was not a happy camper. I was even less happy when later on in the day, I realized there had been a different bus drive by that would have taken me to work with a transfer, but it was a different route number, so I didn't take it. Is there another bus or route I could take? What a great question that would have been rather than waiting and being cold.

During that same time waiting for the next bus, I decided to go to get a coffee across the street. I only had debit, no cash. They said they were sorry, but they were in the middle of a power outage due to the snow. The coffee had already been made, but they could only take cash. So there was the storm, the bus and now no coffee. Shortly after realizing I could have taken another bus, I also realized I had a free coffee coupon in my wallet I could have used. I didn't need cash or debit. Is there another way I can pay? Is there another option available? If only I had asked different questions that morning, I would have had such a different day!

Where is the God-Factor? Do you keep going around the same mountain, or does the same thing keep coming up whether you read the paper, have a conversation, or go somewhere? It may be that God is trying to get your attention. He may be trying to guide you in a certain direction. It could be a direction you never thought of before.

He may be telling you to pray or take action in some way. Is He saying something to you? What is God doing in your life? Sometimes we may not get the big picture, but we will get a sense in our spirit that there is something more than what we see. We may get a sense of knowing in our spirit about a certain person, opportunity or person is in our life. It's not a coincidence.

Watch to see where God is working, what He is doing in your life, and how He is directing you. Is He working on forgiveness, trusting, loving, or building character in your life? Is He opening doors or closing doors? Before I moved to my present location, I lived in four places in four weeks. It was a bit much as it involved a layoff, a flood, and also a trip to the hospital among other events. When I found myself thinking there was nowhere for me to go, I woke up to the fact that the doors had closed to that place and season. It was time for something new. God was moving me forward. I had dreams of being closer to family and other thoughts lying dormant which seemed to spark to life. Within weeks, I was living that dream out halfway across the country.

There are divine assignments, divine connections, divine conversation, and divine timing interwoven throughout our everyday life and events. We also have an enemy who comes to kill, steal, and destroy everything from our hope to our very life. It is wise to ask God for discernment.

If God is involved, it will be for good in some way, shape, or form. If there is destruction or death with no good thing evolving, it is either of the soul realm or the demonic. Pastor Will Sohnchen says it's so important that we understand and know God is a good God. If we don't understand that, then we cannot trust Him. If we cannot trust Him, we will not be able to love Him or receive His love. We will want to hold back. Fear and doubt will speak.

I've learned that God's direction is always for my protection and blessing whether I can see it at the time or not. I've learned to trust Him with what is unseen to the human eye, unheard by human ear, and not understood by human reasoning. Sending His Son Jesus was for us to have eternal life and to have a personal relationship with Him. If you haven't asked Him to be part of your life, that would be a great place and question to start with now. He can give us a peace that far surpasses any situation or place. His peace is one of the best ways to discover His perfect answers to the questions we ask in life. In fact, He can give you some questions you've never thought to ask before.

Will you let Him also help you, help your thoughts to move—and move you forward in the process to Life Beyond Stress?

11

The Journey Continues

I've shared these things with you to give you your own tow truck when you need it. A tool kit of questions to move and fix those dead-end thoughts and live in the stress-free zone of life!

There are a couple other things to be considered with stress cycles. Often, we keep doing things because they do work for us in some way and are meeting our needs even if it's in a dysfunctional way. If you have a hard time letting go, you might need to ask and consider what is it that you think or feel you would be missing if you don't let go? What are you interpreting it to mean if you actually let go? Is it true? I knew an older woman who interpreted worry as love. She thought she had to worry because it was part of caring. She also thought if you didn't worry about her that you didn't love her. It created a lot of conflict between us. I had learned to be aware of the real issues, make decisions that were within my control, pray, trust God, and let the rest go. I could love her and be worry-free!

There is also a time when we have to apply pressure against the pressure we are experiencing in order to break through. Both the caterpillar in the cocoon and the chick in the egg are at first in a place of comfort, safety, and growth. There is space. As they grow, however, they will start feeling the cocoon and shell as uncomfortable and limiting. There may be a tendency to try and shrink in or away from what now seems restrictive and uncomfortable. At some point in their growth, it's going to feel like they are in a very tight squeeze as space and movement are reduced, and the pressure builds. In this case though, they need to apply pressure against that pressure, to keep at it and keep going until they break through to freedom. To have someone come and just pull them out may seem like a compassionate and kind thing to do. It would be the worst thing possible! It is in the pushing, the struggle, the time and effort that they become strong enough to break through and strong enough to deal with what's on the other side.

Likewise, we sometimes just wish or pray that the situations and what's around us will go away, or that we could escape. However, if you become aware of where you are, what's going on, and what you have at your disposal to break through, it will become easier and quicker to break the cycles and live beyond the stress.

Remember, questions are the answer.

In the quality of questions you ask, will be the quality of life you will live.

I'd love to hear how this book inspires you or helps you along your life's journey. I pray it's just the beginning of a phenomenal life for you! God bless you and help you to live your life beyond stress!

To check out other products, read my blogs, leave a comment or request life coaching, please visit my website at *Livingfree.tateauthor.com.* I look forward to hearing from you!

Coach Margaret

Part II

Be Still and Know:
Moments of Reflection

1

Our Journey

No one else can live our life or walk our journey for us. In spite of what others think, say, or want, you are the only one who can be you.

God assures us that He is with us, beside us, and within us. It is His heart to guide, direct, lead, help and equip us for each step along the way if we let Him.

Think for a moment of standing on the sandy beach of an ocean. There is beach as far as you can see. Beyond the shore you see water until it meets the sky. Across the ocean is a different world of nations and people. Looking up, you see the vast horizons of the universe where galaxies undiscovered await. Behind you is the past that led you to this place and moment. There is the past direction from where you came, the past time of years and events, past places you have experienced, and the people who have been part of that journey. There are also footprints in the sand—your footprints that time and tide will wash away.

Think about the school where you started grade one. For all the students who are in that school now, do they know that you were there in that same classroom or chair? The thousands, if not millions, of footprints you made going in and out of classes, day in and day out for years are gone. The evidence that you were there is the progress experienced and lived which brought you to this place today. At some point in the future, what will be the evidence that you are standing here now at this moment on this sandy beach called life?

As you look around, what do you see? What does this place where you are mean to you? The horizons of the future beckon you from every side. There's a destiny in every direction. Where will you go from here?

2

Shelter

"He who dwells in the secret place of the Most High shall abide under the shadow of the Almighty. I will say of the Lord, 'He is my refuge and my fortress: my God; in Him will I trust'" (Psalm 91:1–2).

In shelter there is protection from destruction. When we dwell and live in the consciousness and presence of God, we are protected, we are sheltered, and we can thrive. It doesn't mean there aren't stormy situations or circumstances, but their effects in our life are limited. Our life has been preserved to this moment, and we are still here, while some are not.

The difference between protection and shelter can be like that between a breeze and a hurricane. It can be the difference between feeling the heat and being scorched.

When we dwell somewhere, it refers to our home where we belong; not those places where we visit or pass through. It is a refuge from everything outside. It can be a haven from stress, chaos, the cares, concerns, and effects of the day.

Living in God's presence is where we will be at peace, feel at home, and know we belong in our spirit. There's freedom there. When someone is lost, they seek shelter. Refugees and people experiencing war seek shelter. Birds and animals seek sheltered places to nest and have their little ones.

God says "Seek and you shall find." Seek the peace and refuge of His presence, His Word, His wisdom. Where is your shelter and safe haven? Let Him be your refuge, strength, and dwelling place—a higher place—wherever you are.

3

Clarity

In clarity there is order, insight, definition, understanding, and focus.

When you are driving in heavy rain or snow, there's little visibility or clarity. You can't see the boundary lines on the road. You may not be able to read the road signs, know where you are, what direction you are going, or what's ahead. When winds hit the river, the mud is stirred up, and the water becomes murky. You can't see anything clearly. A lack of clarity or sight is the definition of blind. It's a disability. When you can't see clearly, you are disabled, limited and restricted.

When there is confusion, when life situations or circumstances seem murky, when emotions are stirred up, when you're not sure of your direction or your next step, sometimes the first thing you need to do is nothing. Just wait. Wait for some clarity. Wait for time to reveal some truths, bring focus, insight, light, beauty, wisdom, answers, and direction.

To step into murky waters, you are unprepared for the unseen. You cannot judge, see, or know where it is safe or where danger lies in the currents. You are unaware of the depth and drop-offs. That is a dangerous state to be in.

Wait, pray, seek good counsel, find the facts, seek truth, look for your options, as well as listening for what gives you a sense of peace in your spirit are ways to begin getting clarity in your life.

4

It's Not Too Late

It's not too late to ask for help.
It's not too late to finish something started long ago.
It's not too late to reach out to someone.
It's not too late to make a wrong right.
It's not too late to start over.
It's not too late to do something that will make a difference.
It's not too late to pray and get the power of God involved.
It's not too late to learn something new.
It's not too late to live your dreams in some way, shape, or form.

Sometimes the people, places, ways, and timing of dreams may change, but the essence of your dream lives on and can come to pass in many ways.

Perhaps certain people have passed away, certain businesses are no longer in business, or you're not at the age at which you wanted to experience something. God can cause other people to come into your life, new doors of opportunities to open and other places to appear on the horizon. You may find that doing something now has more meaning and value to you than it would have before. You are more capable, mature, appreciative, and wise. Right now couldn't be a better time. It's divine timing.

It's not too late to get back up. Arise!

It's not too late for restoration in your life of health, relationships, finances, and whatever you feel has been missed, taken away from you, or destroyed. God is in the restoration business! He makes a way!

It's *not* too late!

5

Stillness of Morning

In the quiet stillness of morning, a new day dawns. I don't know about your life, but in my life there are no trumpets heralding each new day. There are no fireworks celebrating its presence. It silently arrives.

No matter what the circumstances, situations, or places, a new day begins.

There's something so peaceful to be in a place of nature and just be enveloped, surrounded, and embraced by the peace and beauty of dawn. It's good for the soul to connect with that quiet stillness and beauty. Likewise, in our spirit, we need those "dawning" experiences to awaken, find, experience, and live in the quiet stillness of God's presence and voice. To be at peace, to be still and open to the greater realm of spirit in which we live and have our being; to be sensitive to the Spirit and what God is saying, teaching, or showing us. It's in the quiet stillness that we become conscious of being one with God. We awaken to the wonders of His Word, the preciousness of His presence, and the quiet confidence we can have in Him. We can sense the peace, love, majesty, and power of His spirit in our lives and journey. We experience the realness of being able to rise above this natural realm with all the cares and demands of life.

As dawn breaks, be still, be renewed, be at peace, be empowered to go forth into this new day fully alive and aware of God and all His goodness and the blessing and beauty of life.

6

Fruitfulness and Abundance

From the beginning of time, God has called His people to go forth, to be fruitful and multiply.

Through wars, exile, captivity, and many situations in which they had to be delivered, survival was their prayer. God's true desire for them was for fruitfulness, profit, value, increase, and expansion—not just survival. Part of God's blessing to Adam and Eve was His spoken blessing and command to them to *be* fruitful and multiply. When Jesus saw the fig tree with no fruit, He cursed the tree. He was not happy with lack.

Sometimes we get stuck in survival mode, lack or just getting by. Where are you? What have you gained from the time you have lived, the effort you have given, the work you have done, the relationships you have made? Is there progress, growth, and development?

Ecclesiastes says we are to have and enjoy the fruit for our labor. It's a spiritual and natural law, similar to the law of cause and effect or sowing and reaping. Abundance is also seen in nature. An apple has many seeds in it, but can you ever fathom how many apples and future trees will come from one seed once planted? It is a continuous process. There are seasons for planting, seasons for nurturing and growing, and seasons of harvesting the fruit. There are seasons of resting, where on the surface nothing seems to be happening, but inside there is still life. With time and patience, there will be growth and fruit once again.

Fruit is created. It grows. It's a process. It's part of life. Fruit is not made by human hands or manufactured in a factory. Multiplication is a great spiritual law and principle. Multiplication is abundance. What is going to multiply in your life this year? Persistence? Joy? Peace? Progress? Skills? Prayer? Victory? Be fruitful and multiply!

7

Places

Geographical places. Emotional places. Mental places. Relational places. Financial places. Spiritual places. Heavenly places.

The Bible refers to pleasant places, wealthy places, holy places, and resting places. There are places of beauty. There are places of strife, confusion, devastation, and negativity. There are places of love, friendship, abundance, growth, happiness, relaxation, and success. Most of these places are destinations we've arrived at.

There are places of hills and valleys, forests and prairies, mountains and oceans. These places are places we experience as a journey—places we go through, as a route, taking us to a specific destination.

We get to places by choices, steps, and decisions. Except our birthplace, places don't come to us. We find ourselves in places that we have journeyed to.

Where are you now? Is it a place you enjoy and would like to stay? Where is this place on the map of your journey to where you are going? Is it a resting place? A stopover or destination? Are you like a citizen, or a visitor in this place?

There are divinely appointed times and places when we know we are right where we need to be for the time. There are places where God has opened doors for us and led us. It is a place of blessing, a place of God's presence, and a place of peace. Those places are like heaven on earth and so worth the journey!

8

What's Around the Corner

None of us know what the future holds, or what's around the corner in our lives, home, family, work, and country. In spite of that, we make decisions today that will influence and create our future.

A choice may be activated when we become aware of a need, situation, responsibility, or opportunity. We act on it by planning, speaking, doing, or getting involved in some way. We make decisions regarding that awareness.

Another choice is to ignore, put off, excuse, deny, or avoid our awareness. When we choose this path, it's likely that someone else will actively take the opportunity or responsibility, and we will experience the results of their decisions. That's the result of our choice to choose the path of least resistance.

To be passive because we don't know what the future holds is like saying we're not going to work, home, the store, a friend's house, or on vacation because we don't know what's around the corner. Even if there is an accident, a train, an avalanche, a large animal, construction or some-thing else we can't see, it doesn't matter. We can't make a choice about what we don't see, don't know, don't hear, and don't have.

Right now, we have the choice of this moment. It's very simple. What's your desired destination? What's the first or next step to move you in that direction? You can choose what to do with the finances you have right now, the time you have now, the opportunities you have now. Position yourself better for future days and opportunities. Choose the rest of the journey once you get going. Whether you continue as planned, make changes, add, or eliminate something. Maybe you choose a different direction, a faster lane, or more relaxed and scenic route.

Make decisions to keep moving forward. Live your life instead of fearing or worrying, feeling like a victim and missing out on a fulfilling future. Be part of creating the future and life you want.

9

The Unexpected

Unexpected moments. Unexpected places. Unexpected results. Unexpected people. Unexpected things, events, blessings, and challenges of life.

They take us out of our comfort zones because they are usually beyond our control or choices. If we knew, then they wouldn't be unexpected. If we could control them or choose them, we would have planned for them.

To this I say, embrace the blessings, the beauty, the help, the joy, the goodness you can find in the unexpected.

Gold is hidden in the earth as are other precious gems. Little European dolls are hidden and placed one inside the other. Within our lives, the moments are within the hours, the hours within the day, the days within the week, the weeks within the months, the months within the years—and all of these together within our lifetime, creating our life.

Can you look through the unexpected with a sense of anticipation? God says His ways are not our ways. What is in your unexpected moments and events of life that is like a treasure with much value? Can you see evidence of

God in it in any way? Are there unexpected opportunities in disguise?

Even if the unexpected seems negative, is there a lesson to be learned, an opportunity, a warning or a change to be made? What can you mine from that dirt? I always think it's rather awesome to see a little sapling tree pushing through the cracks and crevices in the most unexpected rocky places.

The unexpected, when given time, process, and consideration, can be a blessing with surprising and unexpected benefits along our journey.

10

Not Moving

Driving down the highway, I saw a crow standing on the divider line, eating something. I assumed he would get out of the way as I got closer. He did not budge. I thought I'd clipped his wings as I went by. I looked in the rearview mirror, and he was standing seemingly oblivious.

> "I have set the Lord always before me; Because he is at my right hand. I SHALL NOT BE MOVED" (Psalm 16:8).

That crow didn't care what was coming at him; he wasn't moving. He was going to guard what was his. He wasn't giving up. He wasn't going to be moved by me coming toward him, or "the fact" that I was much bigger than him. He was determined to stand his ground. As long as he was standing there, no one else could stand there. We need to do that in life.

We have an enemy who comes to steal, kill, and destroy by circumstances, thoughts, threats, intimidation, words, and fear, to name a few. God has given us vision, instruction, wisdom, and many promises that we can stand on.

They will change facts, cause us to walk protected, live in blessing, and help us stand our ground. Taking these things into our thoughts, mind, and spirit and speaking them are ways we can "set the Lord before us." It allows Him place, permission, and something by which He can establish us. Distractions, circumstances, and whatever else the enemy would try to throw at us then will not have power in our life to move us. We are established in God's strength, way, truth, light, and power. We shall not be moved!

11

Riding the Waves

We can choose victory rather than being a victim of defeat. Jesus spoke to the storms. He calmed the storm and stilled the raging sea.

When the waves of life come crashing against you, when there seems to be a tide of things coming at you, and when the billows roar, is the storm speaking to you, or are you speaking to it? Jesus talked to the storm and said "Peace, be still." What are you saying?

Will you be like surfers who ride the waves going up and over them instead of being overtaken by them? They use the waves as a means to take them somewhere. They've envisioned and learned how to maneuver over and through the surrounding waters.

Use the word of God. James said even though there are great ships driven by fierce winds, yet they are turned with a very small rudder. Our tongue and words are like the rudder in our life. They can change and set the course of our life. God is my deliverer; in Him do I trust. No weapon formed against me shall prosper. No evil shall come near my dwelling. How can those words change your life, your emotions, your future, and the situations in your life?

Use the spiritual surfboards of prayer, hope, trust, faith, Godly counsel, and listening to the Holy Spirit's leading and wisdom. Surf the waves of life, calm the storms, and allow them to be part of progress in your life.

12

The Impossible

"With men it is impossible, but not with God; for with God all things are possible" (Mark 10:27). "If you can believe, all things are possible to him who believes" (Mark 9:23).

What in your life do you feel is impossible for you or to you? What keeps you from believing? What thoughts or desires have you left behind, let go or given up on feeling that they're impossible?

Sometimes we don't believe because we think we're the ones who have to do it, control it, or get it perfect. Sometimes we've put limits on what we think is possible because we don't see beyond how we think it should come to pass. Jesus only said *believe*, and in turn it would be possible. He didn't say we had to know all the details or be in charge. Many times, scripture refers to God causing things to happen, to change, or to come to pass. That "causing" is divine intervention. The when, where and how are up to Him.

"As you know not what the way of the spirit is, nor how bones grow in the womb of her with child, so you know not the works of God who makes all" (Ecclesiastes 11:5).

Part of "believing God for the impossible" in your life is to realize that He is divinely working and intervening in situations, timing, people and places for you. He is doing something within you, developing you. The divine is eternal. There are no expiry dates, natural time limits, geographical boundaries, or age restrictions as He continues to work in your life. Ask Him for the impossible! Expect the impossible!

13

My Path

"You will show me the path of life. In your presence is fullness of joy. At Your right hand are pleasures forevermore" (Psalm 16:11).

Do you realize that no one can say they aren't on a path? A path is the route and the steps you are taking. Just living as you go is still a path you are creating in the process. It is taking you somewhere and will continue to take you somewhere. There's a destiny to every path and journey, even if it's a dead end.

As soon as you tread on grass, in mud, on sand or in fresh snow, an imprint and impact is left where you have stepped. A path is created by steps taken. Sometimes the path has already been created. Sometimes we are on a unique path of our own in uncharted territory.

The more often you travel a route, the easier it gets to walk that path because a way has been cleared, packed down and becomes more like a road. What routes do you take most often in life? Prayer? Faith? Fear? Doubt? Self-centeredness? What routes have become ruts or addictions that you need to get out of? What step would take you in a new direction and path?

> "Behold, I send an Angel before you to keep you in the way and to bring you to a place which I have prepared" (Exodus 23:20).

Sometimes we want to take shortcuts or easy paths in life, but as the name indicates, you are cutting something short—you will miss something in the process. On God's path for our life is the provision to walk that path. God desires to show us His path for our lives. What is the path He has and is showing you even for today?

14

Morning Glory

Put your face to the sun.

How often are you aware of the beauty and fragrance of a flower or a scenic landscape being present at night? In spite of their reality, when darkness comes, the beauty is unseen and hidden. If those flowers and all the life present in the landscape are kept in darkness with no light, all would perish. Light is a source of life.

God is light to our spirit. God is life to us. He is the source of life itself. Without His presence, the beauty, growth, and fragrance of life cannot come to fullness in our lives. Too long without the source of life means death and perishing, not just eternally, but in this life. We wilt and become weary in the process.

What a waste it would be for a garden to be planted and then left in darkness to perish.

Cloudy, overcast days bring some light. Moonlit nights bring some light, but it's only in the full light of a sunny day can beauty touch us, encourage us, and inspire us. After a long winter, what a joy it is to get out on a warm spring day when everything is coming to life again.

Find some sunshine and live in the light, both physically and spiritually. Find people of sunny dispositions. Find the sunny places in life. Where can you, or what can you do to put your face in the sun and let the light and love of God shine on you, in you, and through you today?

15

Finding the Honey

What are you feeding and dwelling on? What thoughts and emotions are you thinking and feeding on? Bees feed on and harvest nectar that will bring forth honey and sweetness to many products, tables, homes, and lives.

As a man thinks, so is he. The bee searches for what will produce honey. Seek, search, knock, and ask. What word from God can direct your thoughts and steps today? The mind is forever thinking, but we do the searching; we have the choice of content.

Conversations, thoughts, knowledge, entertainment, people in our lives, literature, pastors, friends, family, various means of media, the Holy Spirit, and the Word of God are some of what feeds into our life, mind, and spirit.

What are the boundaries for what you feed on in your life? Even our garbage collectors and dumps have boundaries for what garbage they allow. Toxic items, chemicals, and explosives are to be disposed in a safe manner so as not to contaminate the whole dump. Stop and think about that one—not contaminating the dump! If a dump has boundaries on garbage, shouldn't we, as a reflection of God, made in His image and living in His presence, choose wisely what we feed on and give place to in our life? What is the vision, purpose, and mission for your life that needs to be nurtured, fed, and cultivated? What encourages and moves you to that place?

Seek and find that the Lord is good. Let His beauty, ways, thoughts, and desires bring forth sweetness in your life. Whatsoever things are lovely, pure, and of a good report, think on these things.

16

Listen

Stop! What do you hear? So often, we are surrounded by noise. It can be good noise, annoying noise or noise we're so used to that we just tune out. Sometimes we are so busy and distracted that we miss what's really being said or going on around us.

More importantly, do you hear what your heart, mind, and spirit are saying? What thoughts keep coming back? Do you hear some answers? Do you hear what your heart is reflecting to you? What's important to you? What's bothering you? What do you need to check, change, or even invest in with time, money, or effort?

If you silenced all the voices and demands around you, what would you hear? A message? A direction? A warning? An insight?

Clear away chaos, distraction, and noise. Stop and listen. On a full moon-lit night down by the lake in the country, I can hear the water gently lapping against the shore, crickets singing, and other sounds of nature. I hear harmony. I hear peace. I hear thankfulness from within me for beauty, for life, and for a God who has so blessed me to be here at this moment.

What do you hear God saying? He speaks in many ways. Through our spirit in thought, through His word, through other people in our life, through situations, through those knowing senses, through messages we get along the way by what we observe, experience, hear, and sing. There's great value in hearing what God has to say: wisdom, understanding, protection, blessing, instruction, life!

Stop and listen. What will you hear beyond the noise?

17

Balance

When things are out of balance, we can feel overwhelmed, weighed down, tired, burdened and unknowingly wonder why.

God created balance in creation. We need balance. When the load on a forklift, vehicle, or weigh scale is off-balance and too heavy on one side, those things are going to roll over, fall down, or break under the weight. The unbalanced weight may hold for a time, but then something gives. Balancing a checkbook ensures what needs to come out of the account matches the balance in the bank, eliminating a lot of unnecessary trouble and costly bank fees.

When you feel overwhelmed, drained, or burdened, do some balance checks. Do you have a healthy balance of time for work, time for play, time for yourself, time for others, time for the demands of natural life, time for sleep, time for spiritual and natural rejuvenation? The book of Ecclesiastes tells us clearly there is a time and season for everything in our life. Do you spend too much time inside and no time outside in the sun and fresh air? For the negative aspects in your life, have you got corresponding positive people, places, and insight to balance you out?

If someone breaks their leg, often a crutch or a cane is used so the weight and work of the body does not overload the other leg. Sometimes to put balance in our life, we need help, tools, strategies, wisdom, or someone to come alongside us and share the burden. Some cares we need to cast on Jesus and let Him turn situations around for us. Some cares are just responsibilities that we have to tend to, which we can find better ways to handle. Making a list or a schedule can help us implement balance in our life and spread things out so the load isn't so heavy. Where and how can you incorporate more balance in your life?

18

God

"Give unto the Lord, O you mighty ones, give unto the Lord glory and strength. Give unto the Lord the glory due to His name, worship the Lord in the beauty of holiness. The voice of the Lord is over the waters: the God of glory thunders: the Lord is over many waters. The voice of the Lord is powerful; the voice of the Lord is full of majesty" (Psalm 29:1–4).

The ocean is just a sliver of a glimpse of God's vastness, beauty, power, glory, and majesty. Majesty comes to mind when we see God in awe of who and how great He really is. In the natural realm, there are very few, if any, power systems run by man that don't fail. Hydro and electric systems can black out, blow out, and go down. Machines and parts get worn out and break. Political powers and governments fail and change. Man's words fail because he is man. We lose sight of true power and true majesty. The ocean never runs out of water, and the sun never runs out of heat.

The power of God does not fail, from eternal past to eternal future—there is no measure. "Great is our Lord and mighty in power: His understanding is infinite" (Psalm 147:5). He is above the earth and exalted above the heavens. His words do not fail. How do we find ourselves in the trap of depending, believing, or trusting in man-managed systems? Yet, through the power of His Word, His presence, and His Holy spirit, He expects us to walk in His power in our own lives. Through Jesus, all the power of heaven is open and available to us. "Greater things than these will you do," Jesus said. Are you seeking God's power to manifest in your life? Are you expecting and giving the things of the spirit room and place to come forth from the spiritual realm into your natural world? Open your life for God's "super" to work in your "natural." Go forth in His power, might, and strength.

19

Arise

"And has raised us up together and made us sit together in heavenly places in Christ Jesus" (Ephesians 2:6, kjv).

Arise was a familiar word and concept in the life of Jesus. It was the purpose and desire of His life here on earth for us.

It is throughout the Word of God from start to finish. It's our destiny to arise both now and in our eternal future: arise and have mercy, arise and go forth, arise and walk, arise and walk through the land, arise and be doing, arise and build, arise and anoint, arise and be baptized. Micah declared for Israel "when I fall, I *shall* arise."

Who or what in life gets you down at times? What or where in your life do you need to arise or be raised up in? Where can the Lord lift you up and help you arise?

Arise, look to the hills from where comes your help. Arise, lift up your feet to take the next step of the journey. Arise, lift up your voice, pray, speak up, and share. Arise, lift your hands to bless God or help another just as Aaron lifted up the arm of Moses in the battle when he was weary.

Arise, prosper, move forward, and go upward. Arise, be lifted up out of the pit, out of darkness into the light and heavenly places. Lift up another in prayer or with a kind and encouraging word. Lift up the name of Jesus. Lift up His Word in your life. Honor God. Give Him first place in your life so you can be lifted up in Him. Lift your eyes, your sight, and what you are looking at. Look for the good, the blessings, the hand of God, His favor and power moving in your life. *Arise*!

20

At the End of the Day

Today, thousands of lives will be born into this world. Millions, if not billions, of dollars will be transacted around the world. Wars will be fought, dreams lived, disappointments experienced, and fame sought. Flowers will grow. A baby will take their first step. There will be laughter, tears, hugs, helping hands, and discoveries made, while someone will take their last breath.

In the diversity of what today brings and all you do, what really matters? What's left at the end of the day? Is there thankfulness? Peace? Fulfillment? Purpose? Joy? Love? Are you left drained? Tired? Upset? Stressed? What's left for you and those around you? The tide comes in and goes out, leaving debris and sea life on the shores. The day will come and go, and what will be left in your life? Only what was in the water is left on the shore. Only what is put into a day will be left.

Go beyond just your everyday living and routine. Be conscious and aware of what you experience today. Take time for what matters. Recently, my computer and phone were down for the day. Nothing on my list got done. I discovered at the end of the day that it really didn't matter. I was blessed with time and opportunity to connect with others, get things accomplished that were long overdue, and follow my spirit. Sometimes our lists, programs, and schedules need to be put aside as the Holy Spirit directs us in our day to what really matters; so what's left will be of value in our lives and the lives around us. What will be left after this day, week, and month in your life?

21

Anticipation and Excitement

What comes to your mind when you see these words? If you are expecting and believing good things about your future, then you will anticipate with excitement. If you are expecting, thinking, and believing the worse, you will anticipate with dread.

Focus, perception, beliefs, experiences, desire. We can doubt the truth. We can doubt the lie. We can believe the good. We can believe the bad. When you anticipate, you are expecting and believing "something" to transform from thought state to physical reality. We don't dread or fear the past because it's over. You can't regret the future because it hasn't happened yet. Just because we believe something, doesn't make it true. Just because something appears a certain way, doesn't make it so. The air we breathe and walk through seems transparent to the human eye. Under the microscope, we are likely to see many visible particles and matter in that clear air. What we see with the human eye is limited. We see more through a microscope. We see further through a telescope. Looking through the eyes of faith reveals even more! Faith in the worse or faith in the best; both work! We have choice, and it starts with what we choose to focus on, think, believe, act, and make decisions on.

How about expecting, believing, and anticipating a bigger perspective? A God-size perspective, a God-door or opportunity, a God-thing? Are you anticipating God to do what He says He will do, or only what you would do? He can do exceedingly, abundantly above all we can ask or fathom. He will lift us up. Get the vision of living that kind of life. Anticipate with excitement!

22

Streams of Life

Streams and rain are God's way of transporting life-giving, life-sustaining water to land areas of vegetation and animal life that would otherwise not have access to water. Where there are no streams, rain, or water, there is desert, drought, famine, and lack.

Answers, strength, wisdom, help, direction, encouragement, insight, faith, opportunity, and help are some of what God wants to flow into our life. Sometimes He sends a certain person, a message, or a thought as a stream through which His presence can flow into our life, situations, circumstances, and future.

Have you noticed when rain falls or water pours onto the ground, it searches for a place to flow, go, and travel to? Into crevices, cracks, or dips you'll see it flow. Water may form into a puddle but will eventually be absorbed into the ground or evaporate into the air again. Water is meant to be absorbed into places, people, and things. Our body consists of a high percentage of water. Without it, people perish from dehydration. It's refreshing, cleansing, and part of life in many ways.

Streams are a means of dispersing water from one source and location to another location. Too much water creates a flood, which often means disaster. Streams are the route in which something is channeled, be it water, tears, or other substances.

Flowing water in streams prevents stagnation and contamination. It cleanses and washes away dirt and things that can build up or create a blockage. Drinking from pure streams in the mountains is refreshing and life giving.

What is flowing, trickling, entering, and being absorbed into your life, mind, spirit, and reality? Is it cleansing, purifying, refreshing, and life-giving, or contaminating and destructive? Choose life. Choose blessing.

23

Beauty and Inspiration

What is beautiful to you? There's something about beauty that touches us deep inside and brings forth the oohs, aahs, wows, and look-at-that kind of exclamations.

Beauty doesn't mean perfection. Beauty comes in many ways, shapes, and forms—simple beauty, natural beauty. Thoughts inspired God to action, to speak forth, and move to create beauty: "Let us make…."

There's a mind-set that beauty is nice but unnecessary. But that is not true. Beauty is food for the soul. The opposite of beauty could be ugly. Satan was originally an angel of great beauty, but selfishness, pride, and greed rose up within him. It destroyed him, his place, and his beauty. Beauty enhances. Ugliness destroys; it may destroy mentally, emotionally, spiritually, or physically. An open or exposed wound is not just repulsive to look at. The body has been or still is experiencing destruction. Natural beauty reflects life. Healing is life. Unattended and infected, a wound can cause death. On the other hand, kindness, compliments, and encouragement are forms of beauty that bring life to others and help them bloom!

In the miracle of a newborn baby, the joy in someone's eyes, the majestic beauty of the Rocky Mountains, canoeing on a peaceful, still morning or in watching a deer leap swift and graceful, life reflects and gives beauty. God is in the beauty business. There are many references to the beauty of the Lord in scripture. The beauty of holiness. The beauty in the sanctuary. God makes everything beautiful in His time. Acknowledge beauty in your life today. Recognize the beautiful people, kindnesses and gifts that have been given to you and the difference they make in the scenery of your life. Celebrate the beauty of life.

24

Let Go

In holding one thing, we are often holding another thing. When we let go of the one thing, we'll find we are free from the other thing without exerting any effort or pressure. Change happens; there is a freedom. There is space and opportunity for the new and what we need for now.

- Let go of wrong thinking, and you stop things from going wrong. *When things are going wrong or we don't have peace, it is often a road sign that you may need to rethink a matter or think different. Something's not right.*
- Let go of frustrating expectations, and you let go of disappointment. *It is so important for us to evaluate our expectations in every part of our life. Often it is our expectations that are the problem, not the people, places or things. If I expect a rabbit to swim and a fish to run, my expectations are the problem not the rabbit or the fish.*
- Let go of clutter or stuff, and you let go of chaos and confusion.

- Let go of past failures and regret, and you let go of what keeps you reliving your past. Then you can live the future. You can embrace your future.
- Let go of trying to control everything/everyone, and you let go of being god so God can do His job and be God in your life.
- Let go of "should/should have," and you let go of depression/anger.
- Let go of some relationships, and you let go of abuse and disrespect.
- Let go of the old, and you let go of what prevents making room for the new.
- Let go of the negative and you let go of what destroys faith, hope and light in your life.
- Let go of living in the ideal, and you let go of the deceptive lie of perfection so you can enjoy, live, and appreciate your life and what "is."
- Let go of holding so tight, and you let go of pressure and stress.
- Let go of worry and you let go of doubt and fear so you can trust God, hear God, and have peace.
- Let go of what's dragging you down, and you let go of the chains.
- Let go of what's holding you back, and you let go of what keeps you from moving forward.
- Let go of negative thinking, and you let go of negative feelings.

- Let go of negative feelings, and you let go of negative experience.
- Let go of what/who stresses you, and you will feel and be free.

What do you need to let go of today? What difference would it make in your life, in your day, in your home, in your relationships, and in your finances if you let go of some things? What difference would it make to *let God* bring some changes, to take control and be "God" in every aspect of your life?

25

The Lily Pad

The lily pad is not seen growing in fast flowing rushing waters or in the middle of the ocean. The lily pad is usually seen growing in more calm, serene, and gentle surroundings like ponds.

The progress, accomplishment, and destiny of a ship requires a larger, faster moving source of water. Sitting in a pond, a ship would go nowhere and accomplish nothing.

The lily pad, however, is not usually going anywhere. It grows and lives in the place it's been given. Its place is its destination. Rushing waters would move it, uproot it, and keep it from being established—rushing waters would destroy it.

Likewise, different surroundings and circumstances are needed for different seasons of our life. In seasons of progress and achievement, there can be a rushing and busyness that we sometimes call the fast lane. There are times we need to be quick. Quick to obey a word from God. Quick to go in the direction in which He calls us. There is a need for progress and accomplishment in our lives.

In the fast lane of life we do need to watch that we aren't carried away from what means the most to us and to stay conscious of time—it's a limited resource. We need the "pond" experiences, times, and places along life's journey. There's a need to stay established in our faith, vision, and relationship with God. There's a need to stay in touch with the place and people who give us a sense of belonging. We need to be surrounded by and live in the peace and gentle calming presence of the Holy Spirit through every season.

26

Reflection

Whether we are looking at a mirror reflecting back to us, or considering a situation, time, event, place, or relationship, reflecting can be invaluable. Sometimes it helps us see the big picture, the details or the beauty. Sometimes it helps us make a different decision.

Reflection of the sun or trees in the water is a current echo and picture of their presence in reality, in color, shape, place, and even movement.

Paul said "forgetting those things behind, I press forward," yet he also wanted to "put them in remembrance" of some things. There's value to reflect on the past from where we stand at this present moment.

We don't want to relive past regrets, failures, and mistakes, but we do want to learn from them and reflect in how we would choose to do something now. Even if the past was precious and sweet to us, we really can't go back. However, when we reflect on the precious things of our past, it can renew our gratitude, restore our faith, increase our thankfulness, give us an appreciation for God, His mercy, love, kindness, provision, and the people He has placed in our life.

Without reflection, consideration, thankfulness, and appreciation, we can lose hope. We can get overwhelmed by what's ahead, like Israel in the wilderness. When a need arose, they didn't reflect on what God had done. They forgot. Reflect on how far you've come. Reflect on God's goodness, hand, favor, and presence in your life. Reflect on your journey and all you've seen, learned, experienced, acquired, and accomplished. Reflect on those who have been by your side. Reflect on what life would have been like if these had not been present. Reflect and be thankful! Be blessed!

27

With You

I am With You
I Will Never Leave You or Forsake You

Signed,
God

God of the heavens, God of the universe, God of the worlds unseen to the human eye and unheard to the human ear. A God we can know, whose presence we can feel, whose promises we can experience just as uniquely and individually as the snowflakes that fall.

Traveling through the skies over vast continents, and looking down at earth on a city lit in the darkness of night, how can you fathom the billions of individual lives, each with a divine plan, purpose, and place? How can we truly grasp His greatness, ability, and desire to not just be ever present in our lives, but to be in communication and relationship with us? Or for Him to be part of our lives, and for us to be part of Him? Do we grasp His desire to have an active place in our heart, life, and thoughts? To be our hope, our friend, our deliverer? To be part of our day, trust, plans, desires, and future?

Not just to be present or felt, but to be known. Not forsaken, but remembered, loved, and cherished by us, even as He loves us and said He would never leave us or forsake us.